T0288097

REVELATOR

REVELATOR

RON SILLIMAN

BookThug

2013

LIBRARY AND ARCHIVES CANADA
CATALOGUING IN PUBLICATION

Silliman, Ronald, 1946-, author
Revelator / Ron Silliman.

A poem.
Issued in print and electronic formats.
ISBN 978-1-927040-81-2 (pbk.).--ISBN 978-1-927040-93-5 (epub).
--ISBN 978-1-77166-019-8 (pdf).--ISBN 978-1-77166-020-4 (mobi)

I. Title.

PS3569.I445R48 2013   811'.54   C2013-903858-2
                                           C2013-903859-0

For Colin & Jesse

Revelator is the first degree of *Universe*

Words torn, unseen, unseemly, scene
some far suburb's mall lot
Summer's theme: this year's humid
– to sweat is to know –
pen squeezed too tight yields
ink as blood or pus
so the phrase scraped, removed
offending thine eye: "Outsource Bush"
Against which, insource what? Who
will do it? Most terrible
predicate – high above mountains snow-capped
even in August in-flight motion
picture *Eternal Sunshine of the*
Spotless Mind infuriates many No
action, no funny, plot too
dense to follow, unless (unless!)
mind's eye gives attention First
blackbird signals many (synecdoche)
Bumblebee wonders am I

his flower? One hour shopping
& the vandal's fled – him
we'll know not, never confront
so recall the next day
that anger directed at complexity
as we deplaned in Seattle
old battle never won, never
gonna – sit now still beside
Dungeness River to spot quail
hopping about this untrimmed garden
as dog walkers circle back
jet trails in dawn sky
thread cloud wisps, shadows sharp
in the mountains – pen's cap
placed aloft at the far
end of the shaft, black
ink bleeds into yellowing paper
deep in the fibre, lines
spreading as they dry, hours
harbour us, hold the body
still awhile, eyes, ears, all
fading, as if to withdraw
old ivy hides the fountain
mountain half-peeking thru cedars green
against the morning's pale blue
sky, my fingernail now etched
with a permanent ridge – lavender
as a crop smells sweet
but I'm staring west – southwest

as the sun behind me
rises, cloud catches red pink
then brightens into white – clock
bangs ten at six A.M.
its bell flat – quail still
at the garden's rim, ignores
buzz of red-green hummingbird overhead
– then, minutes later, cloud's dissolved
the near sky bare – boys
by the trampoline in the
dark discuss religion, say *belief*
Here the park faces west
making that Mount Baker, girls
run naked through the sprinkler
neo-retro-pseudo hippies mimic the Amish
sans modesty, boys in tie-dye
skip stones into the bay
Eternity in the present only
I shut my eyes, inhale
deeply to hear five speakers'
simultaneous yatter, squirrels up high
in the cedars bark, dog
golden terrier blend all taut
muscle, sinew o'er bone, jaw
pauses mid-air in flight, just
ahead of the Frisbee's grasp
bi-plane low over the water
now you hear its engine
one sock pulled high – other

low about the ankle – deliberately
I pause two poems, three
pages before book's end, first
growl of plane's motor, sun
higher now contracts shadow, dandelion
froth blows over cut grass
spotted white tops of clover
something deep purple, bell-shaped, nameless
at least to me, iamb
what iamb, chewing endlessly until
I realize I'll never swallow
whatever – jays bark: first fog
is deepest when trail ends
at first bend in the
river – "this in six weeks
will all be swollen, salmon
frantic in their competition," men
also – on the wire-grid doorscreen
various bugs alight at dawn
drawn by the interior light,
something long with wings, something
no more than a speck
with legs, I scream, you
scream, we all scream for
that which is unnamable, unquenchable,
inconsolable (deep in one's chest
surrounding the heart) art is
a mode of stalking, balk
at any configuration, at what's

inescapably omitted, at Monticello I
very nearly wept, to imagine
just once the president as
the smartest, most questioning, most
rigorous of all, no, that's
not it either – seeing (hand
shielding brow) the trail ahead
is empty, the man stops
to unleash his dogs, mist
rises from the river – bland
competency distributed equally among hundreds
begets only rebellion, what winnowing
from the first book to
the next, the nest, mountainside
garden fountain, yellowlegs & killdeer
searching the mud for tasties
"My throat," you say, "is
closing up" but for albuterol
Take a deep breath, sip
tea, someone in the forest
is walking a miniature poodle,
an old woman, now blind
finds each chore takes longer,
an epic quest to fetch
groceries, half a day wrecked
if the doctor forgets to
sign the *Rx*, each walker's
gait, pace is so different,
muscle & skeleton negotiates gravity,

years, teen girl radiates lust
post-Britney mascara hooker look, alongside
a second woman, her grandmother
at the pharmacy pick-up window
in a town so small
Safeway has the lone Starbucks
Eventually books oxidize, words themselves
learn to resist, clouds drift
in from sea, glaciers on
Mt. Olympus visible from atop
Hurricane Ridge, yet the danger
is sunburn, blue grouse startles
up from the reeds, read
valleys below as river's text
now forgotten, stack of books
half-read on the table dwindles,
bald eagle atop cedar rests
just for a moment, *whirligig*
puns up tempest, yes, digit
dig it, always make mistakes
is the program, eagle eye
no good for chipmunk future
slightest morsel, now bluejay loud
in the garden, we've not
yet thought beyond our elders
but to extract the implicit,
soar out over Dungeness River
seeking what? My brother's silent
amid hardscrabble boy's circus, rambling

shadowy house atop dry soil
rain shadow vs. forest's constant
precipitation, atop Olympus 180 inches
per year, oatmeal too thick,
squirrels smaller, hall of moss
coniferous trunk root nurse new
volunteers merge, clinging, seek light
get lightning, river grasses ripple
apple pecked at by crow
Store clerk says "I had
a schizophrenic roommate with a
pet rat named Crumpet" Crescent
Lake's shore so much longer
snowmelt in midsummer, rock face
draped with nets, children scrambling
to ride atop floating log
buys a canvas hat, wide-brimmed
Tip of the hemlock droops
not grown for Xmas, mute
talk of politics, religion
What's thought? What dream? What
half-remembered glimpses from old afternoon
tryst years after more clear
more intense (if that's possible)
absorbed into the weft of
feeling, the dance unveils the text
hidden in space whereas architecture
for the most part blocks
it off (seaplane rises

up off fresh water lake)
Later, Riverwalk encased by mall
nearby the Alamo mute hotels
vacant lobbies tell all, Coke
machine's inner light flicker constantly
the air thick & heavy
clouds scrape o'er flattened landscape
Who here speaks English? Who
hear hark loud as grackle's
incessant laugh battle after math's
ironic sum – economy trumps all
history where now teens cluster
to mock tourism's earnest gape
"It looks so small" because
it is – Trucks evacuating quarry
beep in reverse, diner's posture
alert awaiting omelette, sausages, toast
behind whom the sun arises
white light o'er Morningside Heights
cook hollering to the cashier
in Spanish, then English, then
a third language I don't
understand, cringe before that glare
until muted by cloud wisps
monastic NY hotel room deep
within shadows – What music mocks
its maker? The rope's tug
as Dad shakes his beard
lost daughter found, then sold

into marriage – in walks Burt
again, crossing into language, subway's
stairs become waterfalls under Ivan
until flooding halts commute, what
Milton sees the deaf hear
or knot, cashews, pretzels, honey-
roasted sesame sticks, the earth
below flat & checkered, not
yet autumn (dry desert heat)
Heart races art's phases (hard
faces) heard in place in
pink marble plaza beyond which
red dirt surface of Mars
is not more barren – What
on in or about blazes
molten edge of the sun
spurts – the plane banks left
below Lake Michigan's blue-green
sailboats speckled in the glare
architecture matters when nature lacks
features – Hermes, is it, atop
old Monkey Ward HQ, not
some other Adonis, great brakes
of the wing flaps rise,
indoor heat, door frame's height,
"Swap Swamp Swells" sells all,
tells less, nightmare with flashbacks
figures precognition, people dropping naked
from rooftops ("When I saw

water pouring in, I knew
we were under attack") attempt
to reconstruct the sequence, build
narrative bridge, classic Bob, air
syntax out, neighbour waddles out
to fetch paper, hard copy
is old copy, cold stone
atop which to scoop even
colder cream, white chocolate kisses
battered in, the maple reddens
while the oak goes yellow,
all the others already leafless,
lifeless on the street, yellow
tarp atop the torso, hollow
lung hollers for help, envision
this all without sound sung
deep in glade, inaudible oriole
aria as an arch aches
stretching across its trestle, test
the tree stand's strength before
adding tinsel, glass balls, small
ornamentation, avoid clusters, clutter, dis-
in distribute understood, but tribute?
That is harder, I hear
wheels across the gravel wet
with a dense fog hushed
then digging in to turn
then softer, the newly paved
Goat Hill Road, river makes

a natural border, already icicles
hang in the woods, grey
is the late autumn forest
reduced to branch & trunk
I stuck by the plan
as it by me, hark
as syllables harden, to shape
shifters shaken shine, consonants lock
into crystalline scene, saw
inch from the trunk's base
before setting into water, upright
encircled with light, you stir
"much mice in my mouth"
the bed too firm, impossible
& I too tired drift
book still in my hand
sleep at first sitting, green
encased light over the washstand
behind which thin pipes tangle
into the wall, fog's light
shadowless, soft, the day muted
llamas in the next field
beside the alpaca, the sound
of water in pipes rushing
as others waken, our bidding
or theirs, again to disturb
invokes the lost root, I
sigh, superfluous lamp, light enlarges
an otherwise dark room, winter

sun, smeared, muted, infinite gray-scale
the-night-before-last's luminarias
(Lois, am I leaping?) lit
now only in the mind,
deepset rocker, heavy furnace hum
behind the next wall, camelids
in the pasture turn staring
at the man downhill gathering
patio furniture up in advance
of the forewarned storm, or
you are being driven, along
an unfamiliar route, through streets
of your own former home,
whole neighbourhoods tinged with emotion,
one still dreams of jets
sliding into houses, apartment complexes
gone, one millisecond of stillness
then the heat & burst
an orange ball of flame
explodes in the mind's eye
anxious in your hotel room's
great raft of a bed,
for days the networks discover
new amateur videos, waves far
greater than one can imagine,
on the beach bathers not
even thinking to run, buses
floating through streets of debris
Banda Acch, this week's geography

of the public imagination, Phuket's
stream of tourists washed away,
bulldozers scooping corpses, our newscaster
alone in an empty village,
only the battered mosque remains,
where are the people, how
does this outer life, apocalypse
reported, penetrate my dreams, three
men on the street walking
discussing who will reach 60
when, the way as teens
we spoke of 20, not
even seeing the homeless woman
asleep beneath the newspaper racks
at Mission & Fourth, fifth
of bourbon warms, warns, passed
between three beneath the bridge
day is done, day is
the ever-present challenge, wake
or not, the painter Jess
simply stays asleep, paint hardens
even cracks o'er decades, browns
grow muddy, greens mute, sky
goes pale, in the midst
of an abstract field blue
deep blue squiggles, Don Quixote
approaches, what is possible, seen,
heard, emotive prosody, heart because
it impacts one's breathing, gasp

to grasp the truth of
what is not even visible
cannot be heard, red-haired
setter deaf to the world
lopes slowly, copes by smell
residual sight, my eyes shut
I can taste that I
grew up near, that train's
whistle in the distance unmistakable
– in the fireplace a basket
of dried flowers, green rug
echoes couch & chair, remotes
scattered about, even my eyes
adjust gradually to the light
well before dawn, my lens
instead of an onion, unions
dwindled now to eight percent
in the commercial sector, stairs,
doors groan, the slightest touch
if at night, I wake
by eastern time, street lamp
just visible thru the web
of the plum tree's branches
casting shadow more than light
– okay, what's next? – small plane
audible in the night sky
even before first trucks, first
train, but if you listen
here now is a second,

ceramic frog atop silent piano
not frog but a turtle
describe how shoes scatter, pattern
from happenstance, the way books
stack toward a pyramid always
or else topple (game: Jenga),
crickets for the gecko, biscuits
for the dog, page skipped
is discovered blank, then filled
each word after the other
asserts connection, "conniption" my grandma
loved to say was something
one has not does, already
the fourth train shushes past
Dear Krishna, it's 6:11 A.M.
upstairs a faucet turns briefly
Lilly is grown now, Alan's
hair thins at last, Melissa's
perfect smile still shines but
no sign of Lulu, time
erodes what's dear, what's near
is past too soon to
grasp fully the consequence, dawn
threatens a new day constantly
sun as vicious as dusk
or rather simply uncaring, birds
disinterested in the infant's corpse,
it's language that introduces emotion
or the other way round,

my old street so narrow
two boys throwing a football
would find my world unimaginable
& I'm sure theirs likewise
will amaze them, how quaint
that first home network seems
already, Norma says of Barbara
she's there and then not
mimicking consciousness more slowly now
so that others can see
you feel the heat's lack
but not the wind, wind
up an old clock, airplane
I realize is now tracking
the traffic, the early commute
(first train, best train), still
no hint of sun but
now all the trees, houses
visible in silhouette, the dog
audible by its collar, paws
over hardwood, then a sigh,
across the street windows emerge,
porches, no longer just outlines,
details, a larger jet now
a few cars, then many,
my penmanship more ornate today
no sign of the trembles
an instant ago I sat
in Elliot's kitchen, then taped

words cut from the paper
above the dog's white bowl
"good dog" – the last I'd
ever live with I didn't
know then, I dream you
floating, not plummeting, from high
off that bridge, birds finally
begin to twitter, colour floods
emerging day, the sun still
behind the hills, face west
toward whichever future comes, mockingbird
mimics dog collar, another bird's
three note peep, discern now
which jet is which, pinks
streak the high sky, I
rise, eyes blink shaking sleep
away, 757 angles in fog
bay at the runway's rim
engines roaring, waiting, ready, poised
then flaring, to race forward
up over the salt ponds
half hidden in the mist, silhouette
of the city piercing cloud
(but the bridges are hidden)
inner ear, particular trumpet, displays
pressure, cottony wisps soon scatter
valleys revealed green & gold
I hold the fluted glass
to cleanse the palette, mango

ice cream, or the sauce
hot & sweet, spicy, smoked
eggplant, rice absorbs the broth
breath, breadth, bread, a head
too big for hats, hands
likewise large grasp the ball
with ease, to please herself
she walks on her palms
then flips upright, smiling, sees
more than we know, teases
younger brother, mother, dad, bad
dogs? Never! Invariably dozes, wags
what tale undisclosed in aggregate
fatal to those who, unsuspecting
chose service, fall in Falluja
winter in Chester County, ice
will do it, branches enjambed
snap light's connection, loud *whoosh!*
gives wind voice, chip film
like glass from the walk
watch the car struggle uphill
my hands shaking, the line
shaking, airplane audible but out
of sight, dusk's light alone
by which to write – wait!
Weight will snap the limb
the line gone limp now
hang waist-high, wood raw
at the wound, sun but

streaks reflected to the west
pink-orange fading, blue-white
behind, snow's powder blows harsh
right in the eyes – sinus'
season soon follows, nest high
atop power grid's tower reveals
streaked eye, white head, beak
built for killing, osprey stretches
to observe her world, water
low below great Conowingo Dam,
the far side's a lake
but here what swims beneath
water's surface is easily caught
"no boating beyond this point"
sign in the water, post-9/11
but we drove right over
highway 1, south toward Darlington
country store, a few churches
the fire house brand new
but all volunteer, what else
but sell antiques, old world's
evaporating, not yet new commuters
& a Wal-Mart to transform
these farms into subdivisions, demanding
better schools, a non-laughable cop
to stop emergent crime – stone
said to contain its own
sculpture thwarts choice – to voice
vowels languidly moist lips purse

their part – there's an art
to it intuited before thought
thinks – drone to the fan
in the bathroom, refrigerator's rumble
casting ice, fluorescent bulb whines
in the lamp, damp day
fogs the glass, razorwire rings
the rooftop, the young woman
rises to shake my hand
the helicopter, green, just hangs
high over the gallery floor
The Persistence of Memory smaller
than I'd imagined, the pinks
of the women of Avignon
too bright, I hear morning
as the first siren, trucks cough
paused at an intersection not
visible from here, the blue
of a perfect spring morning
unimaginable above this grey crush
of apartments, who here owns
the slightest yard, young man
alone in Chipotle, chewing thoughtfully
his large burrito, not talking
taking it all in, eyes
absorbing all, could have been
had this taqueria been there
then, myself in 1964, what
little I knew then but

could learn by doing, earn
just enough to eke by, barking
for the Café Wha? dime
for each new customer I
lacked the huckster's flair lone
feather by a gravel road
all one needs by wch
to fabricate the tale, each
to each not beach exactly
but stones against the water
piled up to the dock
beyond which (or wch) mockingbird
hops to confront a robin
squirrel rears up to eat
some morsel in the clover,
each page would blow wild
but for the binding stitched
deep into the notebook's spine
dog barking emerges from barn
but won't approach, such boundaries
visible to the mind but
not physical at all, swan
with a broken wing adopts
small town pond, adapts, adept
at avoiding all leashed dogs
as they pass, as we
far less permanent than this
giant oak not toppled, atop
wch lone raven stalks, wind

rendered visible by the trees
two cardinals buffeted in flight
red messengers their floating text
peeps by, I spy, eyes
pie, terns skim over water
predusk glare over the Chesapeake
blue heron solitary, standing still
osprey's nest looks huge, hum
means mosquito right at ear
rubber soles atop hardwood
screech, scratch, itch, each, two
common terns atop a post
implies a pairing, Jack Russell
terriers under foot but Jasmine
sad-eyed black poodle plays fetch
hard rubber chew toy wet
with success iced tea season
is upon us tall slender
glass but the waiter wears
his baseball cap to accent
Eastern Shore's southern drawl he
recommends black-eyed pea cakes I
think the chutney's spiced marmalade
wake to rain's drainpipe syncopation
to make love at dawn
then drift back to sleep
to rise again still early
enough for breakfast, push window
up for air, Deep Throat's

an elderly embittered bureaucratic hack
is this week's Top Story
to do right for wrong
reasons complicates the tale, today
Fox News wldn't even notice
Language language Allen said Wichita
tape recorder rolling, where Pound
decries Usura white lies lethal
but legal (perhaps) add up
along road to Baghdad Airport
from the Green Zone's barricades
improvized explosive device homemade
goes up rendering hillbilly armour
just so much shrapnel splayed
organs reduced to meat flowering
as consciousness ebbs slow motion
vices become distant instantly echoing
unimaginable in head language language
all the unknown knowables known
not to spark action but
the barn at Wade's Point
in watercolour behind white rocker
mocks time's friction Mrs Kemp
buried somewhere by the barn
but with no stone marker
visible through the reeds, dog
from the red barn barks
empty warning not even rising
onto all fours (for force

fill in all fields completely
fasting, blood fills vial, deep
dark rich red almost black
Blank stares, clinic waiting room
time as emulsion, withhold motion
the nurse has her script
before dawn in the night
woods one imagines Ponge one
imagines anything the steady shrill
scrim of the cicadas' clock's
second hand ratcheting stiffly around
dog in the distance barks
once then is silent once
is not barking but just
to clear his throat – fridge
groans on, its hum balancing
the insect-laden woods, how
many words have I left,
use them wisely, sparingly, each
could outlast me, to what
purpose but this compulsive record
forward from the age of
a small midcentury lad, sitting
cross-legged on my bed, scribbling
anything to be free, anything
to make sense – peel cellophane
from a new tea carton
no indication where it's grown
(Argentina!) no record no ___

sense of the map, Heywood
called his first book *Cartographers*
was there ever a second –
a sense now, over half
a century intricate puzzle
grandmother reduced to ash grandfather
no more silent than ever
just for being dead, sip
today's first tea, the warmth
is the half of it
my throat first craves, table
narrow in the kitchen alcove
West Virginia A-frame cabin, clock
with a different birdsong
for every hour, sans kids
what have you to etch
these words into time, applause
once we crossed the border
my 47th state, family myths
arc over generations, John Franklin
Tansley could not have known
telling any who would listen
that yes the explorer yes
his own grandfather yes but
the grandson Richard goes back
a century later, looks up
finds the marriage record yes
John Franklin yes married Jane
but instead a fishmonger

married a weaver's daughter X
marks the signature, how soon
technology catches you out
these keys enact a surveillance
that will only sink deeper
over time, what you sink
'bout that, from comma to
coma to commerce to con
versus sub jugation the root
marks language's route across form
surname in the family now
just four generations, but literacy
not more than six, so what
arrogance am I then enacting
weaving ink into paper, stains
of a history already blanching
in the light, up above
I hear you stirring, rising
at least to sit up
then slowly, quietly coming downstairs
to use the bathroom, dawn
just starts to be visible
through the blinds, soft glow
neither blue nor gray, sun
not yet visible, they're distinct
sun & the dawn, one
recurs while the other stretches
fans swirl slowly high overhead
but the windchime is still

A stack of new books
awaits on the table, yet
this blue one's a poem
3700 years old – I search
for a tooth sword, voices
carry up the mountain but
the rooster is late, woodpecker
is rigorously insistent, oak tree
hall fell but was caught
by that larger oak, jays
scream in a cluster tho
I see no hawk, lone
natural lake in the state
is in fact a sinkhole
barely visible in summer, what
is to be said for/of
Lost River Valley, towns without
stores, theatres, two schools shut
for want of students, chimes
still for lack of wind,
the part that didn't secede
is today punished for that,
I remember the last veterans
centenarians in the 1950s, then
the last widows (the very
last just now passed on),
in war, between, the cusp
always of the next one,
hummingbird's sense of time, red

at the throat, is that
humans appear in slow motion
even the galloping grey mare
as if thru emulsion, history
is anxiety, breathe here, futures
merge, mock, migrate, mesh, markets
more powerful than Marx imagined,
new forests for old, scattered
brick, metal, you can see
where the garage exploded, compost
everything, at the end of
the Age of Man, gender
intended, drive he said, breathe
palimpsest of loss vs. circus
of denial, ice floes melting
southward to the drain, illumination
alters colour, we need it
but wish it neutral, imagine
night visions not in green
but the muted real, breathe
deeply, air's cold flavour rich
in the throat, the pulse
varies, here more compacted, there
gentle constant throb, each year
this graph shifts entropically, hear
steps slowly on the stairs
coming down, I think of
Dr. Williams carrying his mother
up to bed, I wake

cold yet covered in sweat
this curious organism a shock
to see it reflected, night
windows mock mirrors, our fears
never very far, first require
the new park to evict
465 families, an eye to
"preservation," along the long drive
overlook upon overlook, tunnel thru
hedge with a stone wall
not three feet high, Stonewall
Jackson dragged his troops up
& then over the ridge
down to greet his doom
a death by "friendly fire"
the men exhausted, depleted just
by history, "May you live
in interesting times," to beget
an iron roadside marker, text
to beguile these lordly &
isolate satyrs astride their Harleys
their Yamahas, helmets off now
out for a Sunday ride
cloudless east toward the Potomac
west beyond even the border
once of the nation itself
but not this one, now
we see big Confederate flags
atop trailer homes in gulleys

too close to the road
the multiple half-broken pickups
the likewise multiple dogs but
here a field of llamas
suddenly by our side, blue
state red state what begets
a state, by the road
I saw Lost River briefly
but then it was gone
again, blue tail juvenile skink
skitters across the deck, wind
chimes indoors still without fan,
the farms for sale, how
soon the vast plain of
McMansions, in New York upstate
once we saw antique shops
the kids having moved away
the old houses lean first
before they fall, the barns
testify to gravity's harsh pull
downward, first sun behind maple
too brilliant an orange, too
large in the mind's eye
at the horizon, it both
shrinks & grows pale rising
up over forest, microwave complains
something's been neglected, left bereft
to cool, sun on book
in hand to write, shadows

turn into words if I
but pay close attention, fly
was the origin of faery,
a boy's voice, having yet
to turn, Cove Mountain silhouette
crow before rooster, somewhere distant
a cow & even further
gunfire, what order is there
beyond these faint brown lines
on yellowing paper, old boyhood
secret true at last, always –
Hummingbird still atop branch, shivers
then soars, buzzing rapidly away,
squirrel's territorial chatter, beautiful auburn
spider proceeding intently down fencepost
branch snaps without apparent cause
recognize footsteps coming thru leaves
car rolling slowly over gravel
to where next new house
is being built, roof on
before walls, old PC T-shirts
logos of the forgotten, Hercules
Monographic, Ventura Publisher, Wordstar, Digital
Equipment, Intelligent Electronics, Future Now,
Vanstar, jobs, lives all tied
into such ephemera, this one
works now as an actor,
that one sends me an email
his cowboy band's upcoming gigs

I saw a gig recently
in that basement museum, three
prongs quite sharp for fishing
here in Lost River, hex
dolls & looms, even masks
for besnickeling (trick or treat
as Pennsylvania Dutch Christmas fare)
old photo of a witch
hair beyond her waist wavy
blond or red-blond, octagon
gazebo where a small dog
sniffed me out, roadside memorial
to what unforgotten crash, tended
with care, the flowers fresh
& real, Nancy's daughter Frances
upended in a watery ditch
drowning in not six inches
of liquid, now Nancy's stepdad
on her fiftieth birthday, just
as our shared biological father
on her tenth, seeks fate
as narrative causation, sees faith
as teleological justification, seven days
to create anything, but day
is a human measure, earthbound
not observed elsewhere, if elsewhere
even exists, Intelligent Design so-called
a fraud for the simple
will in time seem quaint

but now attempts to brake
all forward motion, original intent
perceived as denotation, but denotation
is just connotation's special case
all men created equal, literal
interpretation, terrifies homophobes as well
it should, blinds all scroogied
every which way, not light
to flow in, divided, cascading
over table, chairs, humming fridge
until in the skylight's grasp
so much higher, I cry
for the sister I almost
never met, two fans twirling
high in the rafters, slow
circles, cycles, shadowless up higher
than this lamp throws light
birdsong clock limpkin sounds five
Florida brown kin to crane
I've never seen, I scan
foreign films in search of
their birds, no two crows
alike, up here we get
just one hummingbird (ruby throat)
no seabirds at all
ants in the feeder drowning
in sugar water, how different
is that, what other religion
chooses as its primary symbol

an instrument of torture, nail
through the palm, what calm
literally beatific stare, bleeding, starving
"dying of thirst," to speak
well, Benedict, *condensare*, the Vatican
in the grasp of old
fearful men, moth beating wildly
on the window's glass, because
we are heliocentric, we'll confuse
any fool source of warmth –
what is light to this
inanimate chair, its canvas seat
threaded mesh, darkening with age,
light's the breath of colour
but not the source, revelator,
Pound's sphere envisioned, never held
not by him or any
.tho many make the claim
you are not your thoughts
but what then inhabits them
animates them, who draws "conclusions
on the wall," turn off
television, radio, PC, climb up
Seneca Rocks just to look
out upon small river valley
feel the sting of air
deep in your lungs, breathe
is all that is required
until you look around, tricks

pulling slowly north to Moorfield
(up in Petersburg I see
motel called The Hermitage) Monongahela
mountains all about, truck's ribbon
in flag motif type reads
up close "half my heart
is in Iraq," I dream
of Nick Berg often, beheaded
on camera, setting up towers
for radio, a civilian job
his father's eyes haunted now
as who would not, later
these names will mean nothing
names never do, give them
to small-town bridges, schools,
post office, pond, then later
they'll be named again, buildings
abandoned, torn down, our here
even towns dissolve over time
why archaeologists exist, Colin says
"This is my first fossil
not in a museum," ivy
etched in stone, iron goose
balance toy, ran on A-
frame drips in thru skylight
into larger painter's buckets, steady
as a backbeat, clock's tic
faster, softer, refrigerator's constant motor
outside the cicadas are audible,

pulsing, Kitchen Music August 2005,
on top of which, this
felt-tip pen is all
but silent, but my palm
drags softly across this page
left to write, the faucet
also dripping, it's all percussion
save for the fridge, which
has now gone still, cicadas
likewise, the rain now perceptible
thousands of small pats atop
the deck, the roof, this
silence is symphonic, a gamelan
of small effects, John Cage
sits before Schoenberg, postwar LA,
already I'm a toddler, music
means Johnny Ray or King
Cole Trio or the way
Godfrey fires Julius la Rosa
is a scandal, *Hit Parade*
singers cover the top songs
badly, even as late as
the death of Buddy Holly,
the Big Bopper, Richie Valens,
learn to listen, really listen
water accumulates in faucet, then
runs a bit, the nuns
can't dance to it, Jesse
complains bitterly, in a chorus

the one note off-key
is the one you hear
songbird clock announces common loon
the rain is harder now
cicadas back, the refrigerator on
I "tested out" of chorus
only to sing on pickets
to integrate restaurants, Spengers 1965
we shall, we shall not
be moved, just like a tree
standing in the water, we
shall not be moved, rain
now a downpour ceases percussion
almost a string choir (cellos!)
stove's exhaust pipe beats out
intermittent syncopation, listens, trees now
out the window, silhouettes emerging
from invisible night, wind chimes
tangled on the porch, still,
geese audible in the reeds
woodchuck waddles, its body ripples
as it scurries from view
John Brown's so-called fort
small brick building, turned now
in a different direction, 150
yards from its original location
which is now built up
to support the passing trains
hamlet strategic by what definition

that it changed hands repeatedly
during the four-year war
they didn't understand the reversal
using the negative would cause
as a means to position it –
from the overpass we watch,
even talk to the rafters
as they float downstream where
the Shenandoah meets the Potomac
A tall red-haired gal
brandishing her sword-like flute, tossing
it like a baton, Emilian
bagpipes are different, techno twist
to the rhythm, he plays
the conch mindfully, hand inserted
to shape sound, Alison's banjo
fits right in, this morning
low cricket solos, cicadas drift
into daylight sleep, sun reveals
many clouds, mock shark atop
stone wall, you can hear
nearby major road, the air
thick even here, nearly September
faint smell of the sea
each cottage its own flag
ours is the hummingbird, their's
is a collie, flat-bottom kayak
smooth in the water, canals
form a network, 1933 hurricane

punched an outlet, we watch
TV now with horror, water
rising in New Orleans, geese
before dawn already in flight,
somewhere a car alarm, nearby
an air conditioner, old airliner
mounted on an angle, painted
gaudily, around which to construct
a course for miniature golf,
as tho about to crash
on the 14th green, collapse
of all infrastructure, or dystopia
in boats, we all someday
may live in the Superdome,
glossy ibis dark & short
amid all the herons, egrets
scurrying little shorebirds, Mulberry Landing
vs. the dead lying abandoned
on the Convention Center sidewalk
intolerable southern sun, the gulf
now carries its second meaning
forward, N'wlins of the heart
truly broken, the wave smashed
hard against my chest, up
from down means nothing, pull
of the tide back in,
I stood again, my cap
invisible in the green sea
I never saw again, lifeguards

use orange semaphores to communicate
beach shimmering in afternoon sun
one boy builds a levee
only to watch it flood
before the incoming tide, Laura
Bush in Lafayette taking questions
while George seeks photo ops
on the streets of Biloxi
thick lips pursed tight, mock
resolve, somebody's boom box blares
here in the sun, sales
on in the t-shirt shops
end of the season, when
will the geese head south
to what, to where, littler
birds appear to say, hear
robin's distinct morning announcement, territorial
imperative, sun throws first shadows
in sharpest relief, young girls
in their first bikinis prance
(figures of the current dance)
before the lifeguard tower, backs
arched to feign developed breasts
Older gals could care less
& are thereby more substantial
Light before sun, last day
of long summer "season," white
at the horizon turning blue
to the darker west, light

through the trees is yellow
somebody up before I am
traffic crunches on gravel, moths
in despair on porch screen
unable to reach the lamp
Lone large green cricket still
on wire mesh (mish-mash
of graphics party town signage
backlit plastic or neon script
traffic at a crawl, what
parking, theatre's but a shed
we shed our old selves
to enter there, I was
always at a loss, wandering
at night bookstore to café
by spiderlight to autumn's end
the brown downpour of leaves
what yellow stragglers cling, what
new sting in the air
in my nostrils, winter's flare
soon approaches, hostile to colour
& bare flesh, this dish
set upon oak stump
water frozen solid, crows loud
to sight the hawk, squirrel's
odd chattering howl, link ink
but a shadow, think now
letters curl into sound, write
this, old familiar Waterman friend,

the pain in the rein
goes deep into the brain
to form an itch, each
new scratch reawakens what forsaken
light, at once impossible &
inescapable, each boy an individual
the variation untraceable but immediate
grandfather's ears, mother's smile, great
grandmother's abiding dread washes over
yet out the tall window
what cardinals know of history
paired on a branch, dove's
nest resident in rain's gutter
edge of the herd shed
freshest vegetables layered like cake
then sliced, watercress bouquet, three
flavours of butter, then sorbet
just to cleanse the palette,
the arctic char is crusted
more salmon than trout, more
orange than pink, barely cooked
at the centre (I vow
to eat this again), pianist
bangs away at the standards
enthusiasm more than subtlety carries
notes larger than the room,
the log lit at dawn
(wch side am I on?)
the sun at our backs

casts these figures forward, woodpecker
up high among dead branches
history is no more than,
now the log burns down
to write at empire's end
& not know it, knot
too tight, clotted, to pry
loose, *They lost their way*
may be said of us
for want of an enemy
(war equals conflict between states)
but when there is no
opposing power, the fan spins
silently overhead, the log reduced
to a lingering glow, O
damsels in distress *not*, O
infinite need, control, control, contort
this string, lace it up
into a bow (hear *bowl*,
bowel), old owl is not
what it seams, Tobacco Road
literally in Lititz, across which
field lies furrowed, planting ready
high cloudless sky, but birds
everywhere in the leafless
forest, thru which lone stream
draws a clear line downward
to the road, old novel
kicked under the king-sized bed,

the wildness of love, it
never ages, tho we each
prove never the same twice
even over decades, you astride
my face, each taste anew,
gentle bing O my microwave
the heat clings, hill's slope
thru the trees upward, house
atop the hill facing west,
hawk's nest visible now, trees
yet to bud, first greens
on the hillside extraordinarily fragile,
licorice mulch perfumin' the air,
Hindu gal in rural town
working the lunch counter, newspapers
all a day old, the
slowness of cows, men mill
about a Volvo, hood up
right by the on-ramp
every sentence counts, Sara says
book club short story night
O but the poem it's
down to the letter, up
to the sun, I seek
an old feeling learned young
birdsong before sunlight, sitting
cross-legged atop my bed
notebook in hand, the sound
of a long shower fills

the walls of the house
Imperialism for Dummies, our own
best comprador, rug atop rug
shapes the room, to own
at least four sofas, chairs
more than I can count
poor man's dream of wealth
moon most full, audible garden
underneath wood chipper's loud growl
at least a block away
iamb what iamb, cat's fur
over eye's dry surface scrapes
imagine the lens a grape
with the meat & front
wall removed, I dream more
deeply in smaller bed but
upon waking remember nothing but
the fact of it, radio
signals traffic, weather not visible
yet to the eye, I
lean back half-sleeping, boards
groan in the floor to
the weight of each foot,
ankle's title articulates force – to
Google-sculpt for least affect
terms of the search defined
algorhythm & blues, buoy, Bob
on the water, we watch
a race between sailcraft, grey

gulls atop undulating waves, undisturbed
periplum, sun to the east
by definition, an easy familiarity
tho we've not met before
but having read one another
can make assumptions, two deer
I nearly hit, unlit road
just off campus, sliver moon
not enough to see by
but earlier I had found
John's car just by listening
how he crossed a road
& had to walk upstairs
just to get here – lunch
or lurch, wch one? Touch
as if a stone carried
in one's pocket for luck
(or lurk, wch one?) smile
unchanged even thru the beard
the quarter-century, I recall
Robert Kelly large, eyebrows lost
in all that face, instead
he's had to pace himself
against the insatiable, how many
appetites are there, for example
flesh, cash, power so modest
as who should have tenure,
we all struggle equally, each
to her own demons (B.R.

undressing slowly in the window
next door as I stare
filled with terror), the air
carries the train's plaintive call
thru Colorado night, first sound
of movement is nearby door
shutting, motel morning, sparrows elsewhere
in pre-dawn chatter, what matter
history to them, my pen
is all scrawl, what then,
my bags never made it
to the plane on which
I was last to board, beard
yet to be trimmed, turned
shave at the edges, white
ridge, site of black hairs
intermingled, visible only up close
audible not at all unless
you're inside this head, bed
too large but the suite
otherwise crowded, *don't waste space*
hospitality's dictum, location is all
but utilization fosters margins, festering
blister on which to walk
just barely, write by styles
some other night, pen's tip
scrapes the grain to gain
what otherwise is lost, light
thru tinted restaurant window, I

sat alone, this salmon's experience
of this meal is not
my own, lamp or desk
left dark, to avoid glare
prefer shadows, bruise on hip
from cellphone holster, Scotian echo
house amid brambles, great estate
beyond whose gates Oakland's ghetto
beckons, which are the gunshots
come the fifth of July,
constant distant popping, my eye
instead of an onion, Buñuel
waltzing with Plath, imagine her
fused with Frida Kahlo, she
turns & the other also
looks your way, fierce brow's
piercing look, seagull's song here
too deep in the city
to be noticed, trumpet flower
bends to the hummingbird's beak
dipped in, a sound like
tiny kisses, instead of bulbs
Christmas lights in a ball
illumine the room, spool table
few books, many many LPS
each wrappt in plastic, stacked
hundreds deep in six columns
across living room floor, webs
envelop a small bush, signals

what spider, ash dust spread
out over small brick patio,
leaves familiar from my childhood
for which I have yet
to learn names, one boy
asleep on the red couch
not entirely, lets me write
in this groaning wood chair
half-sighs half-snores, inside
my head the chewing's loudest,
once I reach the tea
it's bitter & lukewarm, shadows
cast by the lone lamp
soften as windows announce day
I can hear the hummingbird
but not yet see it
hear the more distant train
that I'll never see, houses
tucked away in weedy brambles
back side of the campus,
I doze sitting up, dream
is instant, we're buying cars
comparing trunk space, side doors
that slide open, young man
runs against one-way traffic
the better to escape, we
anticipate pursuers, they never come,
sausage cut at an angle
perfect for omelette, plane's low,

we're near the airport, windows
shake even before we hear
coughing engine, an intersection's happenstance
your hair shorter, more grey
but the eye's expression unchanging
smile's as distinct as fingerprints,
house sit after house sit
to form a vacation, rise
when it's light, forget television
newspapers, email, instead prowl bookstores
for a day, fly kites
linger over dinner with friends
Jesse prefers the steerhead couch
to futon on the floor
at which distance I hear
BART train's ineluctable hum, toe
almost numb if not throbbing
in middle of foot, horn
of Amtrak's locomotive more distant
each town acknowledges war dead
differently, photos on the news
reflect proud attention, the state
at its most wasteful, save
suicide watch on death row
lives as policy's thoughtless cost,
seals pause at Limantour, heads
(two, three) above water, staring
beach full of sun bathers,
klte fliers, others playing catch

or Frisbee, later we drive
into Point Reyes Station, Bob
Hass reading at the bookstore
while we sip oyster stew
& slice polenta, gibbous moon
waxing large guides us thru
Samuel P. Taylor Park, redwoods
right at road's edge, bridge
back into the East Bay,
hills full of lights, high
up the grade at Marin
(San Quentin, as we pass
is yellow, blending into hills
"golden" in summer, but inside
what most prisoners see, everything's
a dull green (the bridge
asymmetrical & long)), we see
the Bay Bridge thinned, incomplete,
muscle spasm at jaw's root
each tooth in turn askew
a house with an inglenook
camping amid anarchist videotapes, books
arranged by colour, soft purr
of boiling water, old roses
crowded, unkempt, but promises kept
in the Mime Troupe's plot
in the park, I rise
to ice my jaw, sit
in the dark until it's

not, first power tool far
far away, you can tell
just by the whistle locomotive's
speed thru East Oakland, jets
from the airport another layer
hum of BART above ground
then a hammer & voices
none of this is loud
but layers, layers, weaving gently
I can hear my son
breathing in his sleep, hummingbirds
off the balcony, the day
that the Getty announces return
of two pieces to Greece
"acquired without documentation," I touch
the Titanic's wall, steel rusting
encased in "glass," a hole
large enough for one finger
alongside one vast wall's section
in fact just a fraction
the outer wall of two
first-class cabins, c-80, c-81
narrative of artifacts ending here
just 300 specimens from thousands
"rescued from the ocean floor"
(an earlier alcove encouraged, entering,
"Touch the Ice!") pencilled letters
retrieved from leather wallets read
half-legibly 94 years hence, headlines

of old newspapers on sale
in the bookshop, Titanic tattoo
temporarily on bicep will wash
away gradually, Matthew Barney's poor
Styrofoam narrative (goat boys wrestling)
one block away couldn't hold
my son's attention, me either
not when compared to Jess
or R. Mutt, neighbourhood's jigsaw
below before giving way to
checkerboard farms (hills, rivers rip
thru the regularized landscape) fog
translucent over Sierra foothills
clouds more or less distant
compared with the dark smear
further of a forest fire
far to the north, sleep
when you're tired, your body
harbours death just waiting, tumour
the size of a cantaloupe
"not particularly aggressive," I look
for a sign, your eyes
tho tired still shine, smiling
at your own dark humour
eat & rest, then talk
& sleep again, these cycles
foreshorten day, this small house
was smaller still in 1930
two bedrooms, the main bath

added later, backyard non-existent
hospital bed crowds living room
newspapers seem distant now, "Lebanon
Fires Back" in Normal Heights
lowriders blare rap at dawn
sun already hotter than memory
admits, sidewalks wide for tables,
chairs, large shade umbrellas, mango
now is this tea's flavour
(tongue searches gums for oatmeal
which it finds), I search
not to lose you, world
so full of loss, now
kitchen table here in Oakland
(loud quilt hot pads atop
equally loud tho deep blue
plastic tablecloth) I sort
thru dense, intense emotions, lives
we ourselves constructed, the woman
says to Angela Davis, O
I must tell my grandmother
I met you, she once
was a student of yours
(no, Chuck, San Marcos isn't
named for Marcuse save possibly
in some alternative universe), seek
now to stretch time out
each breath forms an eternity
if you inhabit it fully

(eyes closed, ears open), Bina
laughing, her own little joke,
Time to drop the body
soon, maybe not, I should
be blind (may yet be)
should be dead (certificate complete
but for the time, 1947,
lungs clogged with fluid, O
penicillin I owe you, see-
thru plastic orbs even now
Steam from tea cup rises
cup is a glass inside
a hand-sized wicker basket
beside which fortune cookie, mint
a second seed-crusted cookie
watercrafts out the window
bob in their docks, fog
too close this afternoon save
the occasional crazed windsurfer
albeit in a wetsuit
later we find backyard goats
to provoke the neighbour's dog
the girl on the swing
singing to an unheard tune
is older than you think
kitchen snake copper red hisses
the gecko goes unnamed, not
what we had once imagined
we were signing up for

Geese circling over Lake Merritt
audible blocks away, someone coughs
near an open window, man
wearing Giants cap, black tee
Logo just as it was
1958, maybe it's because he
looks exactly like Valmy Thomas
baseball card still etched sharp
red background in my mind
I'm still crossing the street
amid traffic, thinking first pitch
best pitch (but maybe not)
In firestorm zone new housing
expands to lot's edge, but
still I see eucalyptus stands
like dynamite in the woods
ready to be set off
A duck over the Pacific
little bird silhouette against sun
more trumpetflowers up the trestle
how come I never noticed
the years I lived here
cracked Goldsworthy sidewalk to front
the new de Young *Enamored Mage*
new acquisition (amid the birds'
loud morning territorial songs, one
chattering squirrel & a motorcycle
wending up the by-streets, roar
& turn, then roar again,

from down in the flats
you can hear the locomotive
& from a nearby yard
someone clears his throat, pan
audibly fries eggs, church bell
signals hour, ducks call &
the nearby whirr, hummingbird wings)
Nobody's changed houses, 11 years,
one function of economics, remodel
or die, new marble bath
had been the roof, millionaires
on paper barely getting by
the crowded houses of Berkeley
eucalyptus in the neighbour's yard
four storeys tall, slightest breeze
July dawn, perfect Mexican dinner
most tender relleno, black beans
& rice, drag your chair
across the deck, tres guitar
in open tuning, because 3
pairs of strings, Cubano music
from the rural east, west
islands, bridges emerge from fog
swish, swish of analog clock
turns out to be thermostat
try sleeping on soft couch
dawn in every window, outside
someone's alarm rings without end
sun refracted off fog's mirror

hummingbird's kiss, blue ceramic elephant
in bowl of small cacti
half under deck's umbrella, lanterns
sway in slightest breeze, unlit
one raucous jay, beggar's dog
sleeps beside him, another pulls
shirt to cover head, community
mental health, alarm again louder
because door has been opened
tho clock ignored, what then?
Why repair rotting kitchen now?
Why seek, read every book
if the flood won't quit
even when you've left, Desire
Desire is the answer, hunger
never rests, geese each dawn
now for decades circling lake
until day's form is found
all over again, I rise
to write, sun still hidden
behind hills, hummingbird upon branch
appears so still, breathe deep
to taste air, first BART,
first bark, squirrel's tail twitches
causing whole branch to shake
train's whistle deep & steady
three echoes distinct, great shushing
rush of traffic, white noise
forms morning music, outside window

spider quick on his thread
it's all about scale, bicycle's
brakes squeal long way down
Stands on her deck naked
to inspect the day, trumpetflower
pod yellow, almost purple tip
phallic before it explodes, red,
red-orange, bright yellow centre
notebook's pages dwindle, one project
I'll not complete, that's not
its point, but to stretch
even just a little, shape
& dimension, time & dominion,
day's echoes ricochet uphill
canyon to canyon, every fold
marvellous instrument my declining ear
hears what I cannot see,
say, sheer ecstasy of breath
each one, no two alike
ever, audible in head's bell
sinus sounds, own teeth grinding
until jaw's muscles spasm, clench
leaf is not silent, falling
that train is miles away
tho very present, one exhales
before dying, the process complete
Imagine hearing vines, grass grow
it ought to be possible
now sun emerges through leaves

forcing me to turn, naked
gal has stepped inside, ignition
turns, cat meows half moaning
whatever one calls silence, infinite
richness of sound, my own
grosbeak & stellar jay, sun
against granite, whiff of hashish
from the next balcony over
Later they play poker &
have the giggles, Half Dome
half-visible thru these pines
the temperature dropping 18 degrees
to 89 as we drove
up from Oakdale & Taqueria
El Agave (menu's English rough
the food smooth & spicy)
Dawn's song even here entails
layer of constant traffic, birds
familiar & otherwise, mostly unseen
echo also of Yosemite falls
light sharper now, sun above
that stand of trees (Yohemite,
h not an *s*, means
in West Miwok, speaking of
the Ahwahneechee who lived here
at Ahwahnee, "some of them
might be killers"), long trek
up horse poop trail, past
Mirror Lake, not a lake

in summer, to a meadow
right at the base of
Half Dome (or that man,
from the outcrop atop Yosemite
Falls, a rope barely visible
along which a man shimmies
to the main peak, men
die from such ventures, fear
nauseates until he's safely across)
I kill the mosquito mid-meal
on my wrist, hikers posing
for a photo, one talking
still on his cellphone, afternoon
thunder cancels a swim, "What
are you going to do
with that money," woman asks
to boy, "When are you
going to start saving for
a gun," woman speaking Italian
is unable to locate ice,
shows me instead empty container,
dogwood full of grosbeaks, couple
power walking on bike path
just before sun tips up
over peak, sky again clear
after yesterday's rain, last flowers
of a late spring wilting
on the dogwood, new dream
that I'm working once more

in the computer channel, that
we (whomever "we" are) are
about to announce an acquisition,
I'm in charge of integrating
service division, politics in Oakdale
means water allocation, long trek
west from the East Bay,
headlights from a slow caravan
clog Altamont Pass, how far
literally would you travel thus
to work in Silicon Valley,
our raft bobs in water,
a view of the waterfall,
of Half Dome's granite face,
facing backwards briefly, we spin
slowly downriver, or carry
the blue raft ashore (Colin
sprawls across it, half-sleeping, we
dig into snacks, blue chips
not blue at all, discs
of flavoured rice kept dry,
wash the pot left soaking
overnight, sun against east face
of new Emeryville highrise condos
already the hum of traffic
cats and dogs and shadows
of branches on this page
drive slowly by the house
in which I was raised

odd use of the passive
who subsequently has dug up
bones of dead cats, dogs
by the corner of where
the garage used to be
bougainvillea that ate childhood home
any ghost there would be
my mother's mother, unquenchable anger
echoes forward even now, some
of them might be killers
San Quentin's sad yellow expanse
no longer remote, two crows
loud overhead, overheard, what's permitted
to be let in, what
not, neighbour paved his yard
making possible three-point U
before exiting to street, end
of new beginning nears, hydraulic
puff, garbage truck's pause, cans
scrape macadam, the men shout
not in English, I rise
because I can & must
that ink should spread, hardening
into words as it dries
jet flies, speck in sky
catching light on its way
where, Hong Kong, Tokyo, Madrid
words upon paper in atlas
if you choose to believe,

never once went east of
Salt Lake City, but once
to Panama on a cruise
flirting with Virgil Partch, once
with her daughter to Hawaii,
rest easy old ash, golden
urn in Julia Morgan columbarium
her own parents among weeds
just up the hill, fishmonger
figured X to sign name
& thus wed, the sign
on my bumper's been shredded,
the gangster returned to office
for more plunder, four more
pages might be my chant,
every store in Groveland shut,
sign on the saloon, "Bubba,
we love & miss you"
What narrative cut asunder, short
of a proper end, but
ends themselves aren't proper, fixed
image (the camera always lies!)
photo finish edited for content
and to fit this screen,
Scream your name out loud
hoping for an echo, woman
long-time resident takes small steps
walking down steep decline, foot
before foot, thus never notices

hummingbirds in crabapple, deep
whistle of distant train, why
Christmas tree lights about patio
umbrella never shine, ceramic
bowl forms succulent garden, some
bird loud in the eucalyptus
hops about, trumpetflower's cousin
to the fuchsia, "record record
record / attack attack attack," Emily
once said of husband Bob, I
myself might say it now
of any, this included, jot
it all down & never
let it go, the past
never passes fully, leaving scars
accumulate to form a culture
grounded in loss, Dear Los
Angeles Dodgers, my bête noir
not, you form the surrogate
we so desperately need, enemy
enema, it all comes out
in the wash, one road
south of Dogtown, garden fenced
to ward off deer, plums
their skin tart, their flesh
sweet & cool, I almost
don't recognize the hummingbird, still
on the almond branch, farms
here feel vast, we missed

a single turn, Bob speaks
of how *O* becomes *D*
or vice versa, Steve talks
happily of new son, David
& I & ours eat
around a front yard table
just behind a small picket fence
the heat rare even here
you never see birds sleep
hummingbird's red crown, white chest
a view of the bay
from the deck, audible neighbours
not really visible, someone's alarm
reaches endless reiteration, arise, arise
your eyes must be clear
the sound of BART different
from day of my youth
thin haze but no fog
light spreads over San Francisco
clouds at first seem small
until one speck of plane
flies beneath, then a second
absolutely crosswise, big truck's sticker
reads "Give War a Chance"
look for the gun rack
boats sit still in bay
who works there in silence
only because I'm too far
to hear, notebook reaches limit

not unlike mind or heart
whole family singing Beatles songs
as we drive, first thought
not your own, let alone
best, phrases weave against lines
water comes to a boil
squirrels wrestle in the branches
one skitters across the slanted roof
Mount Tam silent as ever
only seems unchanging (human-scale)
clouds above have moved on
leaving new sky, sun muted
still amid trees, I close
my eyes just to listen
laughing jay, distant train, feel
instead air over hair, back
of my hand, its taste
palpable in nostrils, eucalyptus, tea
hummingbird responds to jay, jets
echo heading east, sounds create
(first sprinkler, bottle on table)
sense of my own body
high in the Berkeley hills

ACKNOWLEDGEMENTS

Portions of this poem have appeared previously in the following periodicals: *Blackbox Manifold, Cannot Exist, Dublin Poetry Review, Huffington Post, The Nation, Poetry, Shampoo,* & *Try!* One portion was published as a trading card by Fact-Simile Editions and another as a Wrinkle Press broadside. The excerpt in *Poetry* was awarded the Levinson Prize for 2010. My thanks and ongoing appreciation to all of the editors of these publications.

COLOPHON

Manufactured as the first edition of *Revelator*
in the Fall of 2013 by BookThug.

Distributed in Canada
by the Literary Press Group
www.lpg.ca

Distributed in the United States
by Small Press Distribution
www.spdbooks.org

Shop on-line at www.bookthug.ca

BOOK
PRODUCTION
WAR ECONOMY
STANDARD

Type + design by Jay MillAr
Copy Edited by Ruth Zuchter